HAZEL NUTT
ALIEN HUNTER

BY DAVID ELLIOTT | ILLUSTRATED BY TRUE KELLEY

HOLIDAY HOUSE | NEW YORK

To Mary Martha Beaton
D. E.
For Sundra and Nik
T. K.

Text copyright © 2004 by David Elliott
Illustrations copyright © 2004 by True Kelley
All Rights Reserved
Printed in the United States of America
The text typeface is Kosmik Bold One.
The illustrations are rendered in pen and ink, watercolor,
and giant meatballs (made out of we can't say wutt).
www.holidayhouse.com
First Edition
1 3 5 7 9 10 8 6 4 2

Library of Congress Cataloging-in-Publication Data
Elliott, David, 1947–
Hazel Nutt, Alien Hunter / by David Elliott ; illustrated by True Kelley.— 1st ed.
p. cm.
Summary: Captain Hazel Nutt tries to make amends to the Wuttites of planet Wutt
when her starship lands on their leader.
ISBN 0-8234-1843-X (hardcover)
 [1. Extraterrestrial beings—Fiction. 2. Space flight—Fiction. 3. Humorous stories.]
I. Kelley, True, ill. II. Title.
PZ7.E447Haw 2004
[E]—dc22
2003068595

The starship *BoobyPrize* is hurtling through the darkness of space.

At its helm is Captain Hazel Nutt, Alien Hunter. Her mission? To boldly go where no Nutt has gone before.

"Where are we?" Captain Nutt asks her first mate.

"I'll ask Ralph," says Igor.

Igor turns to the ship's computer. He clicks the right switch on. He pulls the left switch out.

Ralph's lights begin to blink. His beepers beep. His buzzers buzz. Ralph speaks!
"Hello," he says. "This is Ralph. I'm not home right now. But leave a message after the beep. I'll get right back to you. Have a nice day."

"Remind me to get a new computer when we get home," says Captain Nutt.

"*If* we get home, you mean," says Igor.

A huge, round object is heading straight for the *BoobyPrize*.

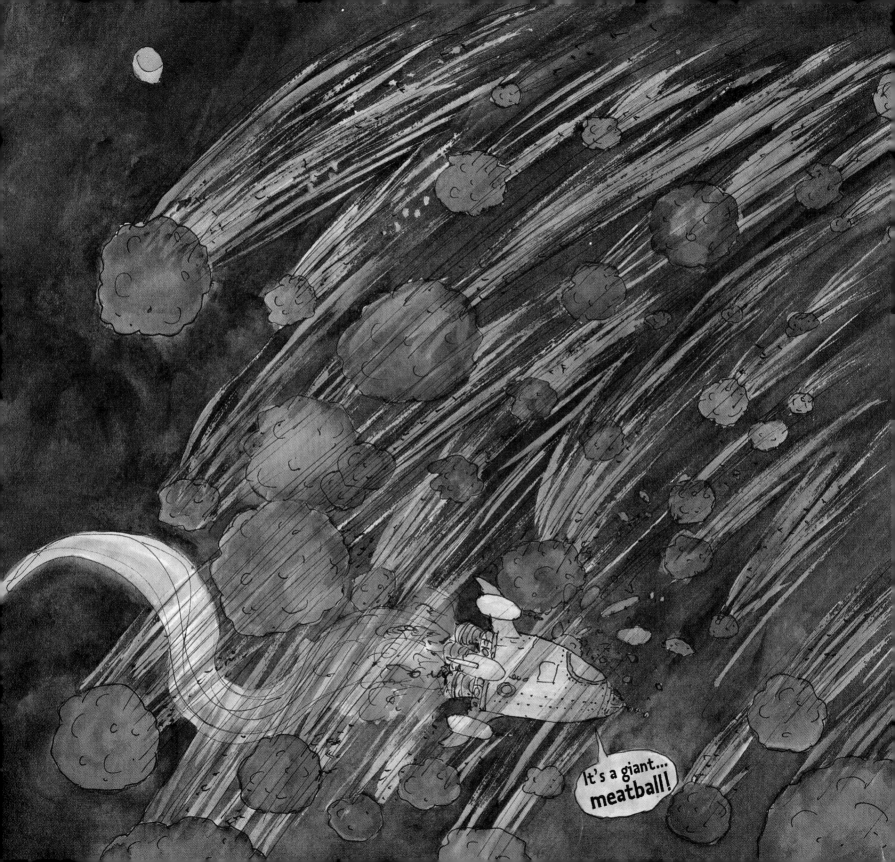

First one. Then another! Then another! Oh no!
The *BoobyPrize* is in the middle of thousands
of flying meatballs!

"This is a disaster!" says Captain Nutt.

"You're telling me!" Igor replies. "I'm a vegetarian!"

"There's only one thing to do," says Captain Nutt.

"Make sauce?" asks Igor.

"No," Captain Nutt answers. "Emergency landing."

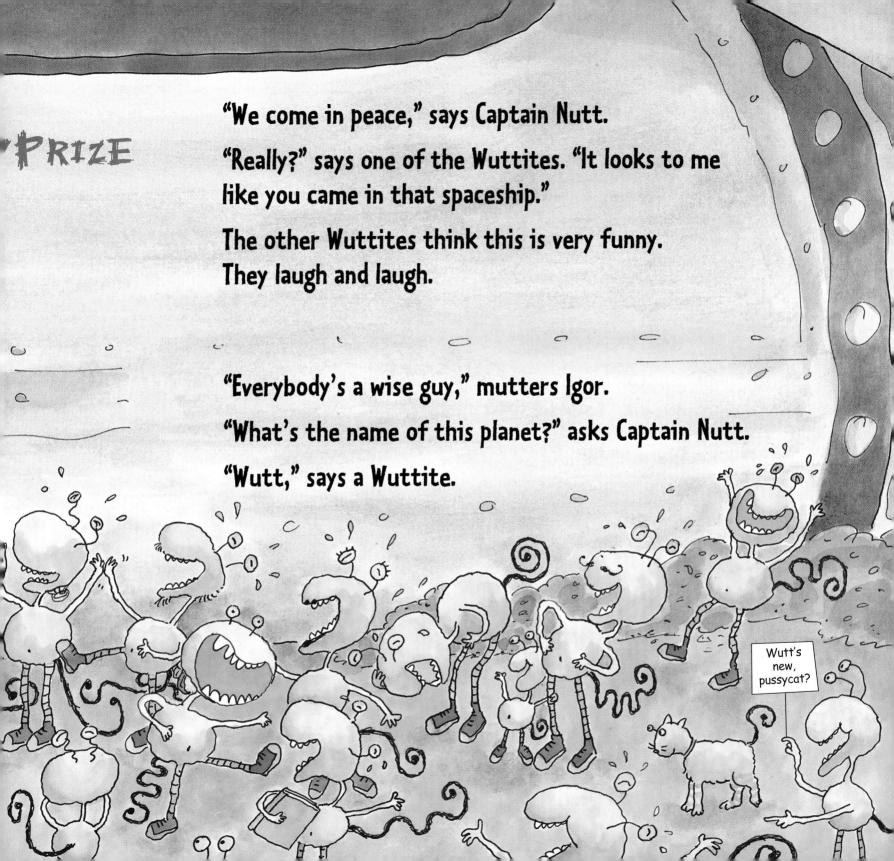

"We come in peace," says Captain Nutt.

"Really?" says one of the Wuttites. "It looks to me like you came in that spaceship."

The other Wuttites think this is very funny. They laugh and laugh.

"Everybody's a wise guy," mutters Igor.

"What's the name of this planet?" asks Captain Nutt.

"Wutt," says a Wuttite.

Wutt's new, pussycat?

This goes on for hours.

"Oh!" says one of Igor's heads. "I get it."

"Wutt *is* the name of the planet!" says the other.

"Well, why didn't you say so?" asks Captain Nutt. She feels peevish.

Wuttever...

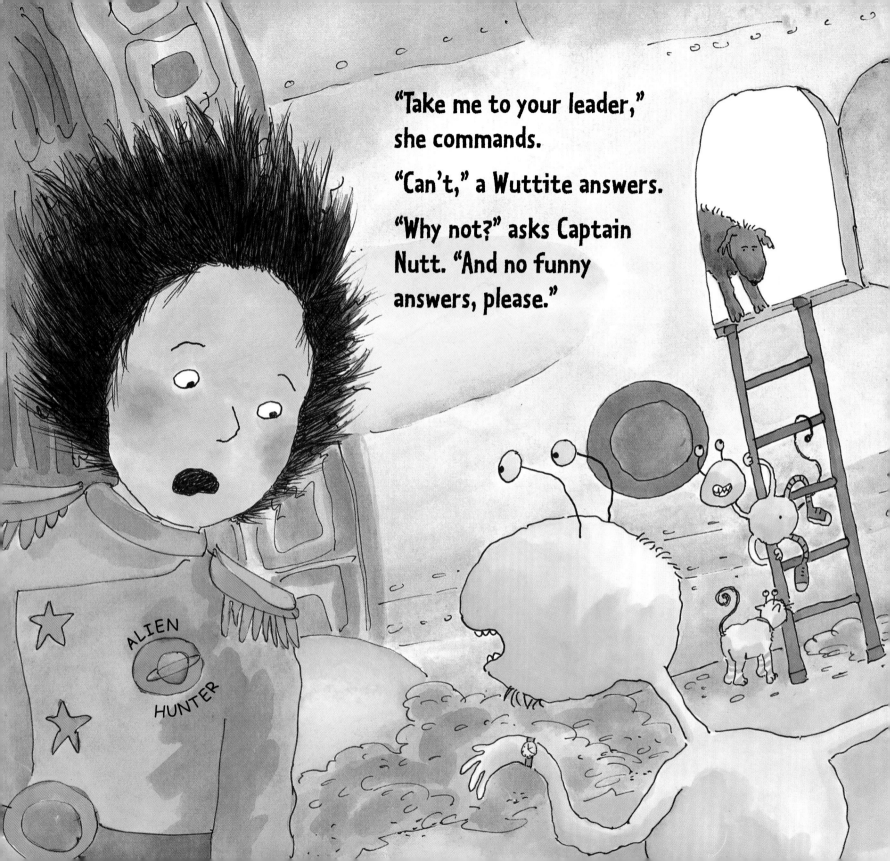

The Wuttite points to the *BoobyPrize*. "Well," he says, "it's like this. You landed on her."

The Wuttites are not laughing now.

"You landed on our leader!" a Wuttite shouts.

"Our *little* leader!" shouts another.

"Our *little lady* leader!" shouts yet another.

(The Wuttites love to shout, so if you go to Wutt, be sure to take some earplugs.)

"Look!" shouts a Wuttite who is holding a large spoon.

"What's that?" asks Captain Nutt. "It looks like a ladle."

"Yes!" the Wuttite shouts. "It's our little lady leader's ladle!"

Suddenly a large object falls out of the sky.
It's one of the giant meatballs.

After lunch Captain Nutt gets an idea. She sends Igor back to the *BoobyPrize*. Soon he returns with a gift.

"It's for you," Captain Nutt says to the Wuttites.

"Oh," they say. "We get it."

"We can't take you to our leader..."

"...but we *can* take you to our *ladder*."

"Right," says Captain Nutt.

"That's the dumbest thing I ever heard," says Igor.

"Not if you're a Wuttite," says a Wuttite.

The Wuttites love their new ladder so much that they hang the ladle on it.

"Look!" they shout. "It's our little lady leader's ladle ladder!"

"Get me out of here," says Igor. "I can't take it anymore."

Captain Nutt and Igor say good-bye to the Wuttites.

"Drop in anytime," the Wuttites say.

Wutt is far below them now. Captain Nutt sheds a tear.

"Do you miss the Wuttites?" Igor asks.

"No," Captain Nutt replies, blowing her nose. "I miss the ladder."